Hinterlands

Published in Great Britain in 2022
by Big White Shed, Nottingham
www.bigwhiteshed.co.uk
Printed and bound by Books Line UK & Totem Poland

ISBN 978-1-915021-09-0
Copyright © Christopher Towers
Cover design & illustrations by Raphael Achache

A CIP catalogue record of this book is available
from the British Library.

for my mother

Introduction

I am passionate about people, place and belonging, about home and what this means, about identity and a sense of attachment. I have travelled around many of what you may call the hinterlands of England, places forgotten or even not known of by many. These places may not always have history and meaning for their inhabitants. There can be a disconnect, as if the places have been abandoned for all except non-league grounds and those that find them affordable to live in, even if their work is a commute away.

My visits to these grounds and towns have often been complex, requiring trains, buses, and maps. 'Getting there' often needed extensive advice from 'locals' to help me find the ground. The fact that locals or apparent locals, have sometimes struggled to even let me know the location or existence of the ground may say something about the disconnect between place and people. That said, those that are associated with these clubs are often 'placed' in that sense and know the club inside out. There are passions also. The game at Halesowen, featured in this collection and titled *Hot Dogs* is between the local side and Prescot Cables. It was infused with passions and set in time with the political reference to the then Labour leader, Jeremy Corbyn.

The game at Halesowen smoked with desire, with some chaos, and that is an important part of the game that I sought to represent. The connections people have with their team are punctuated with desire. Halesowen comes across as a proud club, with history, with its ornate blue gates, standing in a suburb of Birmingham. It was for that reason a pleasure to visit a ground like this and commit some words to the occasion. Passion is similarly evoked at the FC United of Manchester game where the spirit of this team, formed in response to some disillusionment at the modern game and in particular Manchester United, was evident in the banners and singing of the supporters, revealed in the poem *Communion*.

I am concerned to 'say something' about how people live and

how life has changed and in other ways stayed constant but not as an 'insider' to those places, as the outsider, looking in, not in judgement or professing to 'know' what life is like there, but to observe quite literally 'from a distance'. I recall standing a distance from Pontefract Collieries football club and noticing the disused pit shafts on the horizon, a distance away, over a field dappled with stones and heavy turned over soils. The spring sunshine poured down on the stones that formed a pathway to the ground. It made a strong impression on me and my words reflect that.

My feelings about these places include that of yearning, for belonging and place, and one of my poems *Remembering Silverlands* evokes feelings associated with ageing, memory and loss. The football game, high in the hills of Buxton, at a ground called Silverlands is representative of many of these evocations that are about far more than football. There were other times when I simply had less to say, in the poem *Nothing,* centred around a game at Stamford which was devoid of any drama, like many passages of life that are often hum-drum. That needed also to be said, that football in that sense can sometimes imitate life, in its lack of drama.

I often reflected on the meaning of the game for supporters, evident in *Home,* when describing my trip to Hucknall Town and if, or how supporters may reflect on what the team, the club and the ground meant for them. *Rings and Roses,* centred on a game at Coalville, captures speculative thoughts of an imaginary supporter who was reflecting on his marriage as he watches the action. The game at Mickleover, in one of the suburbs of Derby, inspired other speculative thoughts on people, their lives, and their commitment to the game, expressed in programmes and club shops.

Coalville is an evocative ground and I observed pit shafts on the horizon, sitting in the stands on a dark December day. They stood out in the gloom of the afternoon, only fading from view when the sun set over one of the stands. This induced some reflection on the relationship between towns, people, football, and industries lost. Indeed, non-league football encourages wider reflections away from the games themselves. These games have none of the hype of the professional game and capture far more of life beneath the spectacle or the circus. The spectators are closer to the pitch and have more time and space to talk, reflect and observe, free of the hassles of being penned in with many thousands of others in restricted spaces.

The collection of poems crosses two seasons, from the late summer of 2018 to the January of 2020, just before the global pandemic arrived in the United Kingdom. I considered writing background notes to the final poems, written side by side on other pages, to accompany the poems but decided against it as the poems seek to 'speak' for themselves. The poems evolved over time from scribbles in a dairy to a situation where they became publishable, but there was incessant editing to get the 'feel' right, to reflect what I saw and heard. I constantly considered the balance between writing of the actual game and writing of all things other than the match, and the slant is often towards the latter. The game is more than incidental but I am trying to say how much non-league football does not take itself so seriously as the Premier League or even the whole professional game and is often that much the richer for it with stories of many kinds to observe and enjoy.

There are drawn sketches to give visual evocations to accompany the words accompanied by some details of each club, to help orientate you to the club, and its location. All of the twenty-four poems are free verse without any potential constraints of rhyme or other poetic form. I often drafted the poems in one take shortly after attending the game but then worked on re-drafting over weeks and months. The editing of the poems entailed finding words to reflect something more than the games, searching for deeper meanings. The scores for each match accompany each poem and there are references to the play with free kicks and other highlights to recall, but much of each work is about that which surrounds the game. For that reason, the poems may appeal to more than football fans but to a wider audience who are interested in wider themes. All the games are non-league and reflect a passion for the game below the radar of the Premier and other professional leagues. These are the grounds and teams that reflect other aspects of the game, beyond the drive for money and fame. The poem *Khalsa* inspired by Sporting Khalsa, in the West Midlands, reflected aspects of diversity. This Sikh club made an impression, one of warmth and good humour, loads of spirit and pride in the club, despite a lowly status and a day of all-consuming rain. Leicester Nirvana also appeared to be a close-knit club and my afternoon there a sheer joy, observing the pride in a club that is also similarly diverse.

There are also great contrasts in the surroundings or neighbourhoods of many of these grounds with the middle-class affluence of Attenborough in Nottinghamshire to the more deprived Widnes, Coalville, or Basford. The season or weather also added to the different ambiences with the incessant rain at Widnes, on a March day that owed more to mid-winter. I observed that the town 'shivered', which captured my feelings. I recall sitting in a café just nearby the ground, bracing myself for the walk to this huge stadium, more home to Rugby League than football, tiptoeing through puddles and longing for an umbrella. I composed the poems via some notes made in my diary, reflections that became more formed pieces. The notes were often broken down into themes with 'home' always prominent.

The season 2019-20 finished early for football clubs with the global pandemic rendering the games and the season redundant. I recall my last game attended of that 'forgotten' season at Belper Town and a feeling of a 'storm' coming. 'Social distancing', clean hands and with face masks to come, the games ended and there was a feeling of loss. The non-league clubs are often quite literally close to people, where players can and sometimes do mingle with supporters. Grounds are easier to access and the 'distance' of the Premiership to their supporters a vivid contrast. I have had conversations with fellow followers of the game, and their commitment to it is remarkable, many taking long and difficult journeys to get to grounds that are perhaps more obscure and not known. There is much humour in the conversations, often dry. I have heard supporters talk of being proud or even privileged to be at games, at grounds with a wealth of history and tradition. I recall sitting with a man at one of these games with the father of one of the players talking of his son's progress from failed trials with professional clubs and demotion to the lower league. We appeared to come from different backgrounds, but we connected and sat there in glowing sunlight sharing the joys of the game.

The spirit of the non-league is such that it evokes passion and commitment in those that love it, and connection to a game. 'Distance' was to be one of the key words of the global pandemic, but these poems have sought to reflect a closeness between players and supporters, which for a whole season was lost. My poems reflect a range of emotions and feelings, written from a 'distance' of time and place but drawing upon the 'closeness' between the people and the clubs they relate to.

Sporting Khalsa v Long Eaton United
49 Khalsa

Hucknall Town v Basford United
53 Home

Sheffield v Frickley Athletic FC
57 Aerosols in the Stand

Pontefract Collieries v Sheffield FC
59 The Collieries

Stamford v Wisbech Town
61 Nothing

Widnes v Kendal Town
63 Widnes in the Rain

Coventry United v Wulfrunians
65 Listening to the Bells

Harborough Town v Rugby Town
69 Sky Blues

Quorn v Pinchbeck United
73 Through the Trees

FC United v Matlock Town
75 Communion

Alfreton Town v Kings Lynn Town
77 Blue Soft Leather

Wisbech Town v Ilkeston Town
79 Smelling of Winter

Buxton Town 1, Hyde United 0
(August 27, 2018)

Silverlands, Stadium Buxton SK17 6QH

The ground is a short walk from the town centre, up hill from the shopping precinct. There are lots of bed and breakfasts and hotels near the ground or in the town, if you want to go for an evening game and stay over. You can see the high hills over Buxton from the top of the main stand, which is some 1,000 feet above sea level.

Remembering Silverlands

I'll recall
how lovely it was,
watching them
play football,
high in the hills,
keeping summer
companion
on a late August eve,

reminding anyone,
who wants to listen,
as I sit with ragged bones
and stained pants
in a place
known as residential
care.

They will observe closely,
the old folks,
my younger self,
standing tall,
in a stanchion of blue
painted iron,
smiling.

I'll tell them
how Buxton won it
with a free kick,
the ball,
cutting through netting,
almost smoking,
like burning lead
from a crofter's gun.

The nurse
will bring tea
with a look,
of sober indifference,
pretending
she knows me
and that
she's interested
in ramblings
from my mouth.

I'll recall,
walking,
quite freely,
from the ground,
clutching a programme,
watching the sun
turning pink,
one day,
in a place, far away,
from Silverlands.

Mickleover Sports 6, Haughmonton 0
(September 8, 2018)

Don Amott Arena, Station Road, Mickleover, DE3 9FB

Take a bus from Derby bus station to Mickleover and stop around the corner from the ground on East Avenue. It's then a short walk, passing a public house on the way, up the B5020. The ground has an artificial pitch, making postponements less likely. There are a great array of old programmes in the club shop by the pitch side and a friendly, convivial atmosphere at the ground.

Sediments

The programme shop looked like a potting shed,
smelling of dusty old bottles of wine, left over.
Sediments of men, remnants of their younger selves,
fingered old pamphlets with oily, sweaty, fingers.

The sky darkened with cracks of red and flares
of pink and orange as men mumbled about
boilers going on too early for comfort
as they waddled around the shop in fading light.

I watched sports heave balls into the air
as singular looking blokes stepped out from the shop
with wide gaits, hobbling in doughnut looking shoes
and nylon slacks, with socks made for playing tennis.

They held carrier bags from budget supermarkets
full of bundles of old programmes,
destined for sideboards in homes made for one,
as their ruddy faces turned to face the emergent cold.

Their remains of old haircuts swept in the wind
as the home side muscled six goals into the visitor's net.
And as the birds flew over in murmuration, the sky
closed its ranks on the fading sun.

Attenborough 0, Radcliffe Olympic 6
(September 15, 2018)

The Strand, Attenborough, Nottingham, NG9 6AU

Take the train from Nottingham to Attenborough and then a short walk in the direction of the nature reserve and the ground is located at the entrance of the reserve. The club shares the same patch of grass as the village cricket club, with wickets exchanged for goalposts each late summer or early autumn.

Rattling Home

Radcliffe bestrode the village,
laden with jewellery,
draped around necks so heavy
it looked like it needed working hands

strong enough to tuck it between
chest hair and Lycra.
Their shirts shimmered in the sun,
billowing in a cross wind,

with their boots as colourful as
dolly mixtures,
cutting through blades of grass
where red leather cricket balls

and flannelled players roam
when the sun is higher in the sky.
Their shorts tight enough
to upset the vicar

and silence the bells in the belfry.
I sat grazing in sunshine
as Radcliffe rounded rotund villagers.
I swear the chickens clucked more loudly

and the horses neighed
each time the netting sagged, six times,
too many for the villagers,
heading for Beaujolais in the rack,
as Radcliffe rattled home.

North Ferriby United 1, Stafford Rangers 2
(October 13, 2018)

Grange Lane, Ferribly, HU14 3AB

The ground is near Ferriby train station where you can catch a bus or a taxi to the ground or near the ground. The club was dissolved in 2019 and then reformed at a lower level. They play at the same old ground at Grange Lane in Ferriby, playing a few leagues lower in the pyramid of non-league football in England. The allotments at the back of the goal add a homely feel to this club, standing not far from the River Humber.

By the Allotments

The allotments
at the back of the goals
were full of rows
of sprouts,
turnips and swede.

Groundsmen forked
the turf before the game,
draining the water away,
patch by patch,
in high winds

that blew icicles
from the Humber
that twirled in the air,
before landing,
on the pitch.

Each blade of grass,
shining with water,
as spectators
settled with blankets
and chilblains.

Stafford planted two goals,
the Ferriby goalkeeper
removing the ball
from the net
like seeding a potato
with a peeling knife,

taken from slack netting
with a curved arm,
as I tasted salt,
flurrying in the air.

I sat, like an onion
in a bag,
with cheeks
as red as tomatoes,
plump enough
to eat.

Cleethorpes 0, Tadcaster United 5
(October 20, 2018)

Lindun Club, Clee Road, Grimsby,
North Lincolnshire DN32 8QL

The ground is a thirty minute walk along the sea front from the train station in Cleethorpes. Feel the sea breeze as you walk along. There are many places to enjoy typical coastal town food with fish and chips and other offerings.

Sandcastles

A ground fit for caravans,
campsites shops
and chip stalls,
mixing it with
bed and breakfasts
and disused factories,

with the faint smell
of egg and bacon,
sharing the air
with sea salt.
A place where - as a kid
I may have read summer
specials of comics,

bumper versions,
on paper, warmed by the sun,
made for tents,
for summer days,
before the distant
clouds of September
and school.

I recall sand in clothes,
moist bread,
and a need to make the
days last.
But here,
in the Northern
Premier League,

on a day
made for ready rub,
to warm the legs,
I could smell vinegar,

and hear chatter
drifting by the club shop.

Tadcaster raided the goal
five times, smiling,
like kids who'd made a sandcastle,
before the tide came in.

Shepshed Dynamo, 1 Romulus 0
(October 27, 2018)

The Dovecote Stadium, Butthole Lane, Shepshed, Leicestershire LE12 9BN

There are buses to Shepshed from both Nottingham and Leicester, the town is just a few miles away from Loughborough and East Midlands Airport. The ground is tucked away down a side lane from a bus stop in the centre of the town. The main stand is small but cosy as you look down from a good vantage point.

Fireworks

Smells like gunpowder
blew through my nostrils
as I entered the ground they call
the *dovecote*.

Odours like burnt wood
or left-over creosote from a tin,
mixing with what smelt like
old fireworks,

damp, left in the box
for too long,
as I sat there,
expectant,

as the trees swayed
high above the valley,
their branches touching netting,
there to stop the balls going over.

The home side lobbed
a goal between posts,
from a free kick.
The ball guided between the sticks,

evading the goalkeeper
and finding its place
as the scorer
turned to his teammates.

 Looking like a father
standing back from the rocket
as the children enjoyed
the sparks,

before running back
to the safety of the centre circle
with the joyous strides
 of a child,

like he'd defended his family
from a fire,
as others hid in the shed.

Halesowen 3, Prescot Cables 2
(November 11, 2018)

The Grove, Old Hawne Lane, Halesowen, Birmingham, B63 3TB

From Birmingham, take a local bus to Halesowen, which takes around forty to fifty minutes from the middle of the city. The blue iron gates at the entrance to the ground are stunning and there is a kind of bye-gone days grandeur about the ground. The slightly banked terrace is also attractive, spacious and full of charm.

Hot Dogs

Prescot opened the scoring,
almost collapsing the goal
with a football blasted towards
the net, as hot as a pepper.

It started a riot,
the visitors, with hot mouths
and quick hands,
kicking and slapping
advertising boards.

Men,
jostling shoulders
in a sharp wind.
I swear I smelt
gun powder
or perhaps

it was smoke
from chimney
pipes
or hot dinners
from
the suburbs,

as the fans,
rocked
with joy,
humming tunes
of the Sex Pistols
and Jeremy Corbyn.

The away side
led twice
and the game,

rocked like a see-saw
with teams swapping
goals

as I smelt onion
and tomato,
before Halesowen
shot the winner
and a man devoured
two burgers,

with full relish.

Loughborough Dynamo 2, Morpeth 1
(November 17, 2018)

The Newton Fallowell Stadium, 2 Watermead Lane, Loughborough, Leicestershire, LE11 3TN

Take the train to Loughborough, and then it's a good walk of around an hour to the ground or perhaps take a taxi from the station. The only seating is at the end of the ground behind one of the goals. The Club logo is based on the famous Moscow Dynamo side who toured England in the 1950s.

Pumpkins

There was something of Halloween
about the clubhouse with luminous
windows shining with a bright glare
as sharp as light from a pumpkin.

The thick air was so November,
a heaviness that leaves washing,
dripping on lines all day,
the drops like beads on an abacus,

falling slowly to the path.
And under dark skies sparks flew
as the ball crackled between the posts
as Dynamo harried and hassled Morpeth,

not once but twice, the ball twirling like
a Catherine wheel into the net.
Heat seemed to rise from football boots
like vapours from a tray of hot peas,

or from potatoes straight from the oven.
Morpeth, replete in shirts as blue
as pumpkins sometimes are, stole a goal
from nothing,

before the referee blew his cheeks
and then the whistle to leave the
visitors to face the silence of the coach
home, bewitched.

Leicester Nirvana 0, Boston Town 0
(November 24, 2018)

Hamilton Park, Sandhills Avenue, Hamilton, Leicester, LE5 ILU

The club is a few miles out from the centre of Leicester and a bus from St Margaret's bus station, in the city, will get you there.The clubhouse serves a range of interesting hot and cold snacks, including samosa and chips.

Nirvana

I sat like a dumpling
in a stew, left to stand,
sitting in a shed
in black seats,

like a potato in a jacket
waiting for the oven,
for the warmth
of the clubhouse.

I watched Boston toil
all the way from
Lincolnshire,
for this.

The sort of game
that made me feel sorry
for the ball,
leathered,

pumped around
by daft kids and blokes
with wide girths,
and stretched thighs.

Moths and lights,
came to mind.
Going nowhere,
I longed for the end.

Coalville 2, Leiston 2
(December 22, 2018)

Mander Cruickshank Solicitors Stadium, Owen Street, Coalville, Leicestershire LE67 3DA

Take a bus from Nottingham or Loughborough to the bus station and it's then a short walk through some back streets of the town, walking through a shopping complex on the way to Owen Street. The Ravens as they are known, play in a ground that is quite set back from the streets and is surrounded by some fields with an old pit shaft on the horizon, reminding one of the town's industrial heritage.

Rings and Roses

I saw him in the stands,
sitting with sorrow
and tears hanging,
hammock-like, from eyes.
He came to Owen Street
to avoid the missus,
to hide from emotion
and tinsel.

Did he ever love her?
Or maybe it was just
rings
and roses.
His craggy face
looking out over stands
at disused pit shafts,
lit by the moon,

lighting the sky
like a table lamp,
with intense light
amid the black.
Four goals,
each hitting the net
softly,
like warm kisses,

as he smelt
Bovril
in a smoky
charcoal air
as Coalville,
known as the ravens,
but looking like
mint humbugs,

in black and white
shirts,
draped over shorts
as he tasted acid
with a reef knot
stomach,
as he considered,
a life.

Spalding 1, Wisbech Town 2
(January 1, 2019)

Sir Halley Stewart Field, Winfrey Avenue, Spalding, Lincolnshire, PE11 1DA

Take the train from Peterborough and then once in the town head for the ground via the car park that serves a batch of large retail outlets. The ground is only a few minutes' walk from the train station. The main stand is small but charming, looking over the fields in a place known for tulip growing, in fact the club are nicknamed 'The Tulips'.

By the Fens

The pitch looked ploughed
and the players, with faces
as red as turnips, bodies
wrestling like lumps in gravy.

Wisbech started the scoring,
opening the Spalding defence
like a tin of sardines, turning
the defence before peeling away

defenders in the long grass
to score with a razor blade shot
into the slack netting,
as winds blew from the wash.

Wisbech bundled a late winner,
the ball spilling off the Spalding
defender into the net like milk
from a milk carton, opened in haste.

Cold visited my under-garments
as I counted my layers to skin.
The last line of futile defence
against the wind.

The smell of dinner plates and
the aroma of roast turkey,
crackling and stuffing ,wafted
over the stand, piping hot,

with trails of smoke and steam
from houses where people
nursed hangovers with coffee,
and love of different kinds.

Basford 0, South Shields 3
(January 12, 2019)

Greenwich Avenue, Basford, Nottingham NG6 OLD

The club is based, not surprisingly in the Basford area, on the tram stop from Nottingham (David Lane). It is a short walk from that stop to Greenwich Avenue. A plastic pitch, and a warm reception from supportive club staff.

In the Dark

South Shields shimmied on the astro-turf
with purple shorts and faces flushed with
cold, moving like locomotives,
like pumping iron, with steel girders.

Their pale shirts shining in the
kind of light that only January knows,
as if the bulbs need replacing in the sky.

The away side thumped three goals
as Basford pottered around
like middle aged men looking for lost keys,
shuffling on green plastic as if looking

for the shed. The visitors guided strikes
into the opponents' goals, their shots
scorching like scud missiles in a night sky.
It was almost precision bombing.

And as the bright acquiesced to dark,
the nearby tram shone, flickering
like a lighthouse, pulsing, in fog,
like a caterpillar weaving its way,

through soil and grass, snaking,
its way to the city as Basford
looked to the dressing room
for recriminations and showers.

Sporting Khalsa 0, Long Eaton Utd 2
(January 26, 2019)

**Aspray Arena, Noose Lane, Willenhall,
West Midlands, WV13 3BB**

Take the train to Wolverhampton from Birmingham New Street, walk to the bus station in Wolverhampton and then a bus will take you to the ground, situated off the main Willenhall Road, thirty minutes by bus from the city. The cosy clubhouse serves Punjabi as well as traditional English food.

Khalsa

Over a carriageway,
in rain that made water colours
of everything,
I found you, Khalsa.

Nestling in the suburbs
of Wolverhampton,
I found a treasure
in the torrents.

Your clubhouse
standing in a storm as
rain hammered
the roof,

where - men in turbans
invited me to your
home. Their hands
open then shut,

as if in prayer.
I always knew you
would be there,
looking resplendent,

with your stands
of blue and yellow,
ravishing and laced
with a hint of gold,

and jewels of many kinds.
Long Eaton took home
two goals, poached rudely,
as I salvaged two samosas
from the tea-bar,

wrapped tenderly
to not spill
their contents,

encased in a paper
towel, served with care
from behind a bar,
with a kind of loving.

I will remember you,
Khalsa,
not for the game,
but for being there.

Hucknall Town 1, Basford United 4
(March 19, 2019)

Watnall Road, Nottingham, NG15 6EY

Take the tram from Nottingham and get off at Hucknall, the terminus. Walk along the Watnall Road to a roundabout, cross over this and you are just about there, it takes around 35 minutes. Hucknall played the mighty Manchester United here in 2002 and drew 4-4 in front of 1330 supporters.

Home

Even the tea
tasted sweeter than ever
as we sat with our sandwiches
watching men in yellow shirts,

looking as warm as custard
under the glow of giant sparklers
for floodlights,
against the night sky.

Our quiet conversation
about hospitals and appointments
seem as generous now
as the man selling programmes,

with smiles.

And the vibrant jersey
of the Hucknall 'keeper
made us laugh
of oranges

and much of many things,
as Basford
glowed in their piping
white outfit,

scoring goals for fun.
You asked me
if I could get
the shopping for you,

if it became
too difficult.

We shared silence,
and coffee.

Hucknall
was always home,
even if it was
never Old Trafford.

Sheffield 1, Frickley Athletic 2
(March 30, 2019)

Sheffield Road, Dronfield, S18 2GD

Take a train to Dronfield from Nottingham or Sheffield and then a walk from the station, takes around twenty- plus minutes. The Coach and Horses public house backs on to the side of the ground, a cosy pub with hearty meals and ales. The club also boasts a fine club shop with old replica shirts from what is the oldest organised football club in the world.

Aerosols in the Stand

I squeezed through
turnstiles
for the slim or daft,
handling greasy coins,

on a day of bluebells
blooming by the roadside,
swaying in the winds
of March.

The ball pinged between
red and blue shirts,
like bagatelle
under clouds.

Three goals drifted
into netting, like
paper bags in a whirl,
sending the goalies

to the ground
like clothes, tumbling
in a drier.
Sheffield scored,

but Frickley,
blew forward
with intent,
the wind behind them,

as the steam
from the tearoom
made aerosols
in the stands.

Pontefract Collieries 3, Sheffield FC 0
(April 20, 2019)

Beechnut Lane, Pontefract, WF8 4FU

Take a train from Sheffield, to Pontefract Tanshelf (one of two stations in the town) before a walk of around ten minutes to the ground. The power station looms over the horizon from the ground and Haribo sweets have a shop in the town, with a full range of confectionary.

The Collieries

Through a clearing,
beyond some wood,
where the pit shafts stood,
they are playing football,
in the tatters of a ground,
peeled paint on iron girders.

Pontefract has a team
that they still call the
'collieries',
over the slag heaps,
beyond
the disused foundries,

near the sparse
council housing in the valley,
sold to developers,
they dream of new build,
homes on the hill,
with patios.

They play,
with tattooed hearts,
and bodies primed for labour,
but there is nothing here,
no iron or coal,
or brass in hand,

no communal baths
to cleanse the soot,
from scarred bodies,
only a clubhouse,
charred from a fire,
a jape, on a Friday night
that turned ugly.

Stamford 0, Wisbech Town 0
(April 22, 2019)

Borderville Sports Centre, Ryhall Road, Stamford, Lincolnshire, PE9 1US

Take the train to Stamford from Leicester and then it's a thirty-five or forty-minute walk through to the other side of the town. The ground is located in a rural area with a patchwork of fields close by, giving it a very agricultural feel. The ground is a modern structure with seats in a grandstand on one side of the pitch.

Nothing

Like a trip to the in-laws,
the game had to be done,
but there wasn't even a fight
in the sunshine,

in a ground that looked
like a supermarket carpark.
I expected to see shopping trolleys.
But all I could see were red panels,

with a high bank to one side
where isolated grasses
grew around gravel,
with the squares of manicured

fields, yellow and green,
over and above the terrace,
where farmers do their business.
I toyed with thoughts of being

in a store,
buying power tools
or ply-wood.
But love comes in many guises.

I waited for the end
in a game of nothings,
where even a good cry
or a sulk would have helped.

Widnes 3, Kendal Town 1
(April 27, 2019)

DCBL Stadium, Widnes, Cheshire, WA8 7DZ

Take a train from Manchester (or Liverpool) to Widnes and a walk through to the ground, takes just over twenty minutes. The team plays in a huge stadium, holding over 13, 000 fans. It is home to the Widnes Vikings Rugby League Club.

Widnes in the Rain

The Mersey spilled
with rain
as I squelched
into the ground
to see players moving
the ball like a pinball
from feet to feet,

skimming, whizzing,
rotating water.
The ball
spun, like flaying
rain
from a rotating

clothesline,
turning
as if laden
with sodden clothes,
as footballers
spun like Subbuteo players

across a greasy,
rain soaked,
plastic turf.

Widnes flicked goals
into the Kendal net
as the town,

hid behind a plush stadium,
shivering.

Coventry United 4, Wulfrunians 3
(October 12, 2019)

Butts Park Arena, Butts Road, Coventry CV1 3GE

Catch a train from Birmingham New Street to Coventry and then it's a short walk to the ground through the city. The ground is shared with a Rugby Club, Coventry RFC.

Listening to the Bells

I noticed Morris dancers
skipping with bells
and bangles
in nearby side streets,

as Coventry traded goals
with the men
from the Black Country,
in a stadium

meant for Rugby.
The pitch glistened
like new plastic
from a flat pack

as a stranger
bought me a cup of tea
and we shared fragments
of conversation,

like people share chips,
passing words from one
to the other,
as if in ritual.

We sat in a main stand
of blue and white seats
looking pristine,
as if made from Lego bricks,

moulded plastic
just for the occasion,
as clean as car show rooms
and just as shiny.

The chanting
of the dancers
became louder
as they pirouetted

around lampposts
with bobbing head

and bells,
ringing.

Harborough Town 1, Rugby Town 3
(November 9, 2019)

Harborough Town Community Football Ground,
Northampton Road, Market Harborough, LE16 9HF

Take the London train to Market Harborough and the walk to the ground along the Northampton Road is around thirty-five minutes. It's well set back from the road and part of a wider sports and leisure park. A warm and friendly clubhouse where a range of snacks are served.

Sky Blues

The artificial pitch
glistened with rain,
shining droplets
that settled
on a greasy top.

I watched
as patches
of moisture
mottled
my trousers,
making them as dark
as the clouds.

Rugby skipped
over the surface
in light blue shirts.
I hoped
that the sky
might bear
the same colours,

but all I could see
was a collage
of grey and black,
like a pencil
drawing in the heavens.

Meanwhile the visitors
forayed on greasy turf
over the Harborough
defence,
their ankle socks
sinking into boots,
as if never to be found again.

The ball
flew into
Harborough
netting
three times
and all they could do
was celebrate
hot towels
and keeping dry.

Quorn 7, Pinchbeck United 0
(November 30, 2019)

Farley Way Stadium, Quorn, Loughborough, LE12 8RB

Take the train to Loughborough and then a bus from there to Quorn, which takes just a few minutes. Alight the bus near the Quorndon Fox public house on the Leicester Road, just a short walk from the ground on the Farley Way Road, which is a left turn off the Loughborough Road. The club has a spread of lovely tall trees to the end of this neat and tidy ground, housing a plastic pitch.

Through the Trees

The sun, appeared through trees,
an insipid watercolour
as the teams emerged,
with Pinchbeck in pastel
yellow shirts.

Quorn were dressed in a red as vibrant
as hunters' jackets,
as the pale imposter from summer
turned to pink and orange,
in the dusk.

Three goals before the break
as the visitor's defence
was carved open with bodies
felled by the mazy runs of Quorn's
terrier-like runners with the ball.

All this under the spectacle of sunset,
as the legs of Pinchbeck folded like origami.
The ball whipped from boot to boot
to netting, seven times

before I tucked pink hands
into my breeches and headed
for the highway.

FC United 6, Matlock Town 2
(December 7, 2019)

Broadhurst Park, 310 Lightbowne Road, Moston, Manchester M40 OFJ

The tram from Manchester Victoria train station takes only six minutes, alighting at the Newton Heath and Moston stop, just less than a mile from the ground. There is a local café called the 'Miners Bar and Grill', near to the ground, where you can purchase cut-price tasty meals.

Communion

Red, black, and white
banners swirled
over seats
as I entered Broadhurst Park.

The towels and scarfs
and souvenirs
set out like a woven
tapestry,

looking like altar cloths
draped,
to signify a love

at an unseen altar
as flares puffed the air
with lush pink in clouds.
White shirted Matlock

fell to their knees,
hands covering faces,
as united bundled
the ball

into netting,
six times,
in the swirling
fog of evening,

before the whistle
blew
in the chilled air
to signify the end,
as United's faithful
roused a final chorus.

Alfreton Town 2, Kings Lynn Town 2
(December 28, 2019)

The Impact Arena, North Street, Alfreton, DE55 7FZ

Train to Alfreton, on the Nottingham to Liverpool line, and then a twenty minute walk from the train station to the Impact Arena. A small ground with an extra-ordinary amount of seating for such a little stadium, bright red, all along one side of the ground, extending around two thirds up the side of the pitch.

Blue Soft Leather

Kings Lynn, with shirts and shorts,
the colour of sherbet limes,
waded in a treacle of a pitch

as the soft blue leather
of the Alfreton seats
provided vice of a sort.

The fabric, with its
cushioning as finished
as the upholstery

of a show room car
but naughtier,
for its surprise.

I sank into the seat
to witness four goals
traded as the steam

from the tearoom bar
drew men in long overcoats,
queuing for warm comforts.

Four goals
dropped in the nets
as easily as tea bags

in their cups.
Honours even
on the pitch

as the streets
awaited.

Wisbech Town 0, Ilkeston Town 2
(January 25, 2020)

**Fountain Fresh Park, Lynn Road, Wisbech,
Cambridgeshire, PE14 7AL**

Take the train to Wisbech from Peterborough where you connect to
a coach taking you to Wisbech, from there it's either a bus/walk to
the ground in around thirty minutes. The storms of February 2020
demolished a stand at one end of the pitch, at the back of the goals.

Smelling of Winter

I sat in a little hut of a stand
with old bones for company
on a wild day.

Pitching with the locals
on hard plastic seats,
smelling of winter.

The nearby fields
heaving with manure
and heavy soil.

The air was puffed with cold
as I looked for my body
under a coat.

Ilkeston sneaked a goal
between legs and then another
as darkness came

and teeth shook
with cold,
rattling so hard

from winds
from the fens,
on a day for men,

with red cheeks,
and plump girths

and sweaters
wrapped around
bodies as hardy
as old boilers.

About the Author

Dr Chris Towers is an innovative lecturer who uses drama, film and words to support student learning. He brings poetry into the classroom in ways that supported his winning of a major teaching award. He uses poetic expression and composes poems that draw from a lifetime of influences from working with vulnerable adults to composing poems for German and Russian students when teaching overseas. He has honed his poetic craft and developed his awareness of poetry and how to work with it in the classroom through post-graduate study at Nottingham Trent and Cambridge University. It is however his life and work experiences, including travel that are particularly significant, from journeys around non-league football grounds to meanderings through Singapore and Malaysia, from Sporting Khalsa in the suburbs of Wolverhampton to the banks of the Malacca river.